811
P

Peck, Robert Newton
BEE TREE AND OTHER STUFF

BEE TREE
and Other Stuff

books by Robert Newton Peck
A Day No Pigs Would Die
Path of Hunters
Millie's Boy
Soup
Fawn
Wild Cat
Hamilton
Soup and Me

BEE TREE
and Other Stuff

Robert Newton Peck

Illustrated by Laura Lydecker

WALKER AND COMPANY
NEW YORK

This book is for Sarah,
our old barn cat,
about whom I first wrote.

And in fond memory
of Miss Kelly
who christened my paper
with a tiny gold star.

And for a good friend,
Bill Halloran.

CONTENTS

INTRODUCTION

WHAT the heck is a poem? Well, I don't guess there's a more fit describing of a poem than to just say it's a *song without music*. In fact, if you don't believe this, all you got to do is *say* a song instead of sing it, and what you bust out with is a poem.

Like fiddle music, a good poem is a noise you can tap your boot to. There's a throb to it, as there is in your own breast, whether a heart is full of hatred or full of love. Few art forms can keep time to the beat of love or the march of war as well as poetry. Soldiers and lovers seem inspired by pulse, the pain and the passion of a flirt or a fight. Just like a marching corporal, a poet must keep in step and follow the pound of the drum, and yet sing on his way to battle.

Ever butcher a pig?

Hard work. Most farming is. Yet to dirty your hands is a good way to clean your soul. I met a passle of people who have never dirtied their hands, and yet their minds and souls (and mouths) can be so downright stainy that they appear to be lower than dung. I don't guess that farmers appear too poetic to most folks. But every farmer I ever shook hands with has at one time or another spoken a poetic word to my ear. Usually about his burdens or his beasts, his crops, and his land that he works and tends.

For generations, my folks were Vermont farmers. Plain people. A few were migrated Shakers. Others were Methodist and Baptist and Congregational. One was what you'd call a "breed injun" 'and her name was Nellie Saint-John-the-Baptist; so when city folks call me a redneck, at least I can claim it proud. I got born on a farm, and we all hacked a hoe to many a hill of potatoes. My father's neck was red as a raw wind. The furrows that weather had plowed into his face told a solid story, in poetry, providing you got the knack to see fancy when you looked at plain.

That's a poet's job. He must till his land into lines, straight and proud and true as rows of fodder corn to store up in a silo for cows to cud on. And now, even though hard work no longer thickens on my hand, the silo of my pen is abrim with memories to feed my modest herd of readers, providing they can abide a haybarn flavor.

This book could hardly be called literature. Just a chat between friends, you and me. So don't set your standards too high; but instead, put your feet up. Lean back and listen, for I'd be pleasured to tell you about my boyhood and early manhood, and of the folks I knew who helped to whittle me (or warp me). And fit a pen to my hand. They were plain people, so this is a plain book. Crude, raw, unvarnished . . . like biting a dirty potato. Yet if you bite deep enough, the meat inside may nourish you as it did me.

Looking back, I reckon I took a hearty harvest from the earth, as a farmer. As a poet, I share with you this bounty.

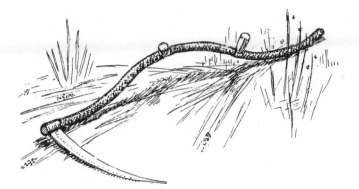

School

MISS KELLY stood as straight as virtue.

With lace about her neck and wrists, she some favored a picture we'd all seen of Mary, the Queen Mother of England. Our ruler ruled with a ruler, in a grand manner, a patrician monarch and a Vermont spinster whose realm was a dirt-road town. Her castle, a wee schoolhouse of red brick. Her subjects were soiled and squirming, often barefoot; the sons and daughters of mill-workers and farmers, clad in faded cottons or handknit wool. Alone, she took us through first grade, second, third, and fourth. For this quartet of years, she was ours and we were hers.

We were unbarbered; and on some hot afternoons, obviously unwashed. There was never a question of authority. We were her kingdom, but she was the power.

"For tonight's homework," said Miss Kelly on that day of destiny, "each of you will write a *poem*."

There was no moan of despair. Only a soft murmur of a reaction to an impossible task; a noise Miss Kelly chose to ignore, as she would any reflexive utterance of digestion. She was quietly confident that we would tackle any request that she presented. Long ago, Miss Kelly had drilled into our heads that a dragon was to be faced, as one must confront a bully, and somehow driven back into the dark cavern of ignorance. Hour upon hour, Miss Kelly read to us stories of noble King Arthur and King Richard, and of Ivanhoe. A snowy saga by Jack London, knee-deep in the Yukon. Plus as much Horatio Alger as it took to churn the curds of childhood into granite chunks of Vermont character.

"Mama," I said as I sat in the kitchen watching my mother pare a wet carrot, "you won't believe it."

"No," she said, "I probable won't."

"I have to make up a poem."

"You do?"

"Sure enough do. Miss Kelly said."

"Well, I don't guess Miss Kelly would ask you to do anything beyond your powers."

"Sometimes she does, to make us stretch our brains. She said that."

"What'll you write your poem on?"

"That's just it, Mama. There's nothing to write about around this old place. To be a poet, you have to live in England, or Boston, or someplace like that."

"You sure?"

"Yup. Only folks that live in here-parts are farmers, like us. Who ever heard of a poemwriter working some dumb old Vermont place?"

"Seems to me," said Mama, "you got poetry a might mixed up with geography."

That was when Miss Sarah, our old barn cat, jumped through the open window and into the kitchen, took a few laps of milk from the cracked bowl behind the stove, and then rubbed her ribs on my mother's shoe.

"Hey there, Sarah," I said. "How's all your new kittens?"

"Seems to me," said Mama, "that a poem ought to get writ on things beautiful."

"Like what?"

"If'n you tag along out to the barn with Miss Sarah here, you'll see."

As it was nigh to chore time, Sarah and I walked through the May sunshine out to the barn. I'd seen her three kittens before; but this time, I took a good look through a poet's eye. Sarah allowed me to pick up each kitten to give it a stroke or two. And right then and there I knew I could do my first poem. Just one look at Miss Sarah and her newborn, and the doggone thing could near to write itself:

Sarah's Wondrous Thing

Sarah is our tabby cat,
And always every spring,
She steals away out to the barn
And does a wondrous thing.

Somehow, she has some kittens
In the hay up in the loft.
They all don't look like Sarah
But they touch so wondrous soft.

Each day I hurry home from school
And up the barnyard path.
And there is Sarah giving each
And every one a bath.

Sarah licks each tiny ear
And tiny tail of silk.
Then they have their supper
Which is really Sarah's milk.

I don't know how she does it,
But she does it every spring.
It makes me want to whistle,
'Cause it's such a wondrous thing.

THE next day at school, Miss Kelly asked some of us to stand up in front of all the other kids to read our poems. I read mine, the one about Miss Sarah and her kittens. It was sort of fun. Soup, who was my best pal, wrote his poem about a frog. The lines really hopped like a toad. After all the poetry got read aloud, we asked Miss Kelly if we could do it again sometime.

"Don't you think," said Miss Kelly, "it would be too much work?"

"No," we said. "Poems are fun."

And they really are, too. But not quite as much fun as girls.

My first girl was Norma Jean Bissell. We had what my mother called a "deaf-and-dumb courtship." Norma Jean and I hardly ever said anything to each other. Our main contact was when Miss Kelly got our class up on its feet to sing all the verses of "My Country 'Tis of Thee." When we got to the line that said, "Thy name I love," I would look with longing at Norma Jean Bissell and she at me. It was the only song we sang that had the word *love* in it. Even now, I can't hear "America" without musical memories of Norma Jean and the singing secret we shared. Later I wrote a poem about another encounter:

Sharing

When first I presented him to you,
You looked as sweet as could be.
You smiled softly and,
Extending your hand,
You tore off his leg at the knee.

I was completely astonished,
Impressed with your cheer and your charm.
When grabbing his hips,
And smacking your lips,
You bit off the rest of his arm.

I wanted to tell you I loved you,
But you would have startled and ran.
Yet you were quite bold,
For just nine years old,
So we finished my gingerbread man.

IT was Miss Kelly who gave us the gift of being able to cotton to poetry and music and art, and to find these treasures within our modest and humble environs.

"You will discover," said Miss Kelly, "that what brings you the most joy in life are things you don't have to buy." She looked right at Soup and me when she said, "You can't purchase a good friend."

That was when Soup (we shared a bench together, until Miss Kelly had to spot us in opposite corners) leaned to my ear and whispered,
"Who'd wanna buy *you*?"

"A poet," said Miss Kelly, "like an artist, can
often see beauty in things that appear dull and
lackluster."

I thought about that, and wrote this:

Dust

Around a distant bend the wagon showed
Itself. And close behind a dusty snake
Was following the wagon on the road.
Not catching up, nor did it overtake.

On the seat, the driver in the sun
Had taken off his coat. His arms were bare,
With sleeves rolled up. A wagon on the run,
Escaping from a snake of dusty air.

As the wagon passed along our farm,
The driver never once did look behind
To see if dusty serpent do him harm;
In fact, the driver paid it little mind.

I watched to see the dusty serpent fall,
As if the wagon had not passed at all.

THE rest of the poetry in this book I wrote at different times in my life, in childhood and in manhood. You may appreciate it more, I believe, if it squats down unedited on these pages just as it oozed from my hand.

Chores

CHORES is a near-forgotten word.

This comes hard to believe, because as a lad, chores made up a twice-a-day ritual that was my farmboy's domain. Papa or Mama rarely had to remind me that it was chore time, or which chores had to be minded. I just knew. The cows, horses, oxen, pigs, and chickens had to be fed and watered. Barns cleaned, eggs gathered, cows milked.

In the morning, chores were performed prior to pancakes; the animals were fed first. And twelve hours later, after school, it was darn near a hanging offense when a boy wasn't home by chore time. Chores wouldn't wait, and woe betide the freckled lad who came home to find Aunt Carrie doing the milking. To me, such an experience happened just once. But never again.

Demanding taskmasters were not only in our barn. Stomping off my boots, entering our kitchen, I'd find another. The most imposing personality in our farmhouse weighed four hundred and twenty pound. It was our old black kitchen stove, a 1901 Acme American . . . six lids, nigh to ten square foot of cooking area. The oven could bake four pies and raise six loaves of bread

all to once. That old black devil sure burned
many an armload of cord:

Wood Box

Behind the old black kitchen stove
Was where our wood box stood.
And as a boy, it was my chore
To mind it brim with wood.

Outside the house, the split was piled
As cut from massive trunks.
Winter ripened, under snow,
In shiny frozen chunks.

But once inside, the sticks would thaw
And ants came creeping out.
The business end of Mama's broom
Would put them all to rout.

Old orchard trees would burn the best,
For after-dinner treat.
And we could smell the souls of apples
Baking in the heat.

Strange, I miss that wood box,
Now I'm growing old.
A house without a wood box
Is just a little cold.

SPEAKING of heat in winter, have you walked into a cow barn on a cold January morn? The animal heat near to gets up on its hindlegs to hoof you as you open the door. It's right cozy. And there is a close kinship between a cow and her milker, no matter what time of year. Looking back, I am grateful the work of milking was asked of me, and even more thankful I had the back to do it. Even at five o'clock in the morning.

Cows get milked twice a day. Funny thing, but morning milking was a whole lot different from evening milking. At the end of a day's work, Daisy, our cow, seemed to know how my body ached with a day's labor, and offered her big warm pillow of a flank to rest me:

At Milking

The day grows soft and pink of sky
To send the old cow home.
To give her milk all creamy white
And rich with butter foam.

There is no sweeter poet's rhyme
Than milking time.

I sit the wooden stool, as she
Stands there in the shed.
And pressed against her silken side
She lets me rest my head.

Far more bless'd than poet's rhyme
Is milking time.

As milkcows sometimes are not always too fussy where they lie down or what they lie on, a good farmer will always wipe off a cow's udder (the pink bag underneath that holds the milk) before placing the milkpail under her teats. If you don't do this, your milk might be rife with a spate of specks that don't do your appetite a whole lot of good. But once I was late for chores, and thought I'd shortcut my work, so I milked dirty. Papa looked into the pail, and then without as much as a word, looked me right in the eye. He never said a syllable, nor did he have to. His eyes said it all. I fetched the strainer.

My father, Haven Peck, had eyes that were kind as could be. But get him doubting, and those same eyes could melt ore. Chances are, you read the book I wrote about him, called *A Day No Pigs Would Die*. Well, up front and before the book begins, there are four lines of a poem. Folks have asked me often if there is more to it, and there is:

Farmer

A farmer's neck is red as wind,
His hair a thicket crown.
A farmer's arms are long and white,
With hands of leather brown.

A farmer's knees are piney knots,
His ankles dark with dirt.
His feet are big and tired slow
And walk as if they hurt.

A farmer's nose is hatchet sharp.
It ends up in a hook,
To almost touch the pages
When he's reading in The Book.

A farmer's back is bent with work
From tending stock and crops.
A farmer's heart will be a gentle
Heart until it stops.

A farmer's voice is rabbit soft.
And farmer eyes are blue.
But farmer's eyes are eagle fierce,
And look a man right through.

I GUESS when my
father saw that I'd milked dirty, he figured that
raising me up to within a loud holler of manhood
would be *his* hardest chore.

Hay

"THERE'S a mite of sweetness in hay," Papa always said, "like you stored away a wisp of August."

It's true. Hay is a very present element in a farmboy's living. Besides being called a redneck and a hick and a rube, a farmer is sometimes referred to as a hayseed. Well, that's right and meet with me. Because I don't guess there's a brace of words in all of the English tongue that can match the goodness and strength in the words *hay* and *seed*. To my ear, they sort of sound like girl and boy. Woman is sweet, like hay, and man is the seed that gives her new life.

Ever see a fresh calf, newly weaned, take her first nibble of hay? Ofttimes you can just hold a bouquet of hay in your hand, and then feel that little nose, all wet and wondering, trying to decide whether it's as good as her old ma's milk.

When a cow or a horse is called a hayburner, it makes reason enough. Hay creates heat. A haybarn on a hot and steamy July afternoon is some kind of an oven; especially if you're loading the barn right up to the rafters. Even the hornets that nest in the beams look hot. And hot tempered, too. Many's the time I had to drive headlong into a mow of loose hay in order to dodge a dose of stinging.

If you're a farmer, you have to know when to cut your hay. Give it enough field time to ripen, so it'll help seed your second cut. First cut is June, second in late August. Not always, though. Hay can be tricky as weather.

Hay is so much a part of a working farm, full of life; and if you stoop down and part the grass, you may be rewarded. The following poem is about an act I saw Papa do. Bless his heart.

Nest

My hay is ripe, and ready to be cut.
Each shaft is feathered out and reaching high
Into the sun. It swishes on my legs.
Some will go to seed before July.

Nesting at my feet, a bird flies up.
She scolds me that my work took me so near
Her nest, and flies about my ducking head,
To beat her irate wings upon my ear.

Below and deep inside the darken grass
Her nest is buried. Now I see it there:
A whirlpool, magic swirls of rounded straw,
Lined inside with down and strands of hair.

[25]

Birdlets four, and all with hungry mouths,
Waiting for a worm, or any bug.
Up they stretch to nibble on my thumb,
Preferring to be fed than staying snug.

With a pole I mark her nesting place,
Remembering to give it widen berth;
So that, with mare and mower, I will spare
The little miracle upon my earth.

NOT all that grows in a hayfield is hay. You'll discover more than birdlets. In the Bible it tells of the tares among the wheat. Tares are weeds. Cows eat those, too. Cows'll eat just about anything in a meadow, even a weed known as a Devil's Pitchfork. It's just a tiny and black two-prong burr, and those wee horns can break off once they're into your skin. There never was a farmboy born who didn't come home with a whole Hell of those pitchforks stuck all over his clothes.

As kids, Soup and I would each pick one, pretending it was a tiny sword so we could square off and fight a duel. Soup would be Errol Flynn and I'd pretend to be Douglas Fairbanks, Jr.

So I just had to write this verse:

The Devil's Pitchfork

August sun smokes hot and mean
Enough to powder dirt.
Loading hay to wagon makes
You sweat right through your shirt.

Your eye begins to wander
And it seeks a sleepy glade,
And over in the meadow
Standing elms make pools of shade.

Beware, you idle farmer,
When you turn your back on work,
And enter dark dominion
Where the Devil's Pitchforks lurk.

They thrive on Old Temptation
And they fertilize on Sin.
And blossom sweet desire
When they see you giving in.

So keep right on with haying
For an eye of burning coal,
The Devil, wants his Pitchfork
Planted in your soul.

OTHER than all those itchy hayseeds down the back of my sweaty neck, right where they'd stick like a brother, and the horns of Devil's Pitchfork poked into my hide, there's another aspect of haying that I will always remember.

It's a sound.

A horse or a team can't pull a mower everywhere on account sometimes the Vermont topography is too uphill or too uneven to allow it. That's when the reaping of hay had to be done by hand, with the help of a long-handled scythe. But hold on! It wasn't the cutting blade that made the noise; it was the whetstone that honed it, that reapers carried in their pockets.

Honestly, if I live to be one hundred, I shall hear this sound ring in my memory. Clank-a-clank-a-clank-a-clank. About every half hour, a reaper would give his back a breather and keen the edge of his blade. Hillside to hillside, the ring of one reaper's hone calling to another across a dell sure sang out a pretty tune. It was conversation among silent men, each claiming he worked as hard as the rest.

A whetstone was about eight or nine inches long. In the middle, it was thinner from wear against the blade of the dull scythe.

The Pocket Whetstone

In the reaper's pocket
There's a whetstone long and gray.
To hone the edge of wonder
As it hones the blade for hay.

When reaper's scythe turns weary
As it sweeps along the ground,
It begs the whetstone go to work
And make its sharping sound.

The whetstone clicks a merry tune
To fill the August air.
It dances in a gown of gray
With pinched-in waist of wear.

You wish to hear my holy hymn?
Come join me in the shade.
We'll reap the blessed rhythm
As a whetstone strums a blade.

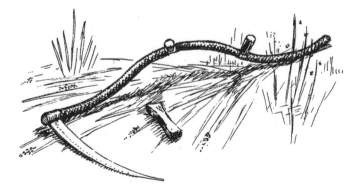

As a boy, as a young reaper, it took more than one field and one crop of hay to teach me how to work a whetstone. But once you master the music of it, your hand can't ever forget the tune.

All of these happenings seem so much in the past, so very very long ago that I have to keep reminding myself that it all took place. Real work by real hands, my own.

Aster

August hay stands ready. Lean and lithe
Vermont bamboo, a jungle of a field.
I, Grim Reaper, with long handle scythe,
Go forth to harvest in the second yield.

I see a lonely aster at my feet.
Six tiny suns, in each a solar shine
And ring of petal rays to give off heat.
A perfect Pennsylvania Dutch design.

I stop. My scythe suspended as a sledge.
Somehow I cannot cut it down. I pause
To take a whetstone out to hone an edge
I just had honed. No reason. Just because.

My scythe's next stroke will make an aster dead.
But it will sweeten butter for my bread.

OF course the final step for hay is when you tumble it down from the loft above your stanchions and into a manger . . . a big trough that holds hay and oats, any dry food for your milkers. It's always a surprise to discover how many folks have no idea just what a manger is or what it does. And I guess I darn near pity any child who grows up without a haybarn to sport around in.

A barn floor made a noise that I'll always hear, whenever a big workhorse would enter. The iron of his heavy hoofs would drum the bottomless boards and really pound a tune. It sang out that the day's work was near to over. Then chores, supper, Bible, and bed.

Old Gray Barn

I walk across a tired field
To greet an old gray barn.
Empty and alone it stands
To spin a yester yarn.

Once, the old gray barn was new,
Its timbers yellow bright.
In between, the morning sun
Stole in with striped light.

Its posts wore round by farmer's hand.
It held the smell of chore,
Heard hoofs of horses, making
Hollow music on the floor.

It knew the warmth of milk cows
With eyes so brown and soft.
It caught the jump of boyhood
In hay up in the loft.

Its land was full of promise
Young and fresh and green.
So rich with August plenty
And all the sweet earth's glean.

The rafters now have swallows
Come to build a nest.
The workaday is over.
Rest, old gray barn, rest.

BARNS hold memories as sweetly as they hold hay. The first time I ever kissed a gal, we were standing in a barn. Well, at least we were standing for a while. Be a pity to waste all that soft hay.

Then came Soup's first car.

Soup and his gal rode inside, but my sweetheart and I rode behind, outside, in a wee little cockpit called a rumble seat. Mama thought that boy and girl were a bit too closely packed to be proper, and she up and said so.

"A rumble seat," said Mama, "is the Devil's playground."

"And back when you were a girl," I asked her, "what was a haybarn?"

"Well," said my mother, "I guess that too was the Devil's playground. But even if our folks didn't know what we were doing, at least they had an idea *where* we were doing it."

Barns hold memories sweet as hay.

Winter

THIS story is probable close to two hundred years old if it's a day:

Seems like there was an elderly Vermont farmer, name of Colrain, or so the story goes. His farm was split over the Vermont-Massachusetts line, until surveyors come by to tell him that his house was a rod or two further south than he reckoned, and that he actual lived in the State of Massachusetts.

"Good," said the old man. "I don't guess the wife or me could of took one more Vermont winter."

Impossible though it'd be to cipher up, I sure would pleasure to know how many hundreds of tons of Vermont snow I have hefted. Adirondack snow as well. Snow may be brutal on backbones, but it's a good quilt for the land. Sometimes when it'd snow late in the spring, just enough to flour the ground, Papa would call such a blessing "poor man's manure," as it was a mighty lean feeding. .

Even though Thanksgiving and deerhunting opened the cold season, winter began in my child's mind just before Christmas. That was when just about everyone in our family started making salt beads. All you do is make little balls of flour-and-water paste; and while they're yet sticky, roll 'em around in some salt. Not table salt. Barn salt has bigger rock-crystals. Then, before the beads harden, punch a pencil or a knit-needle clear through so when they dry there's a hole for stringing, and to trim a tree.

Salt beads sure do glisten. What's more, you can color 'em up yellow (with mustard), blue (blueberries) and red (ketchup).

Mama or Aunt Carrie or any one of my four sisters used to always bake three kinds of Christmas pie. Always the same three: apple, mince, and pumpkin. There's a story about Vermont pie, too. Here goes:

Some folks say a Yankee is an American. But in America, a Yankee is somebody who lives up north. Probable a New Englander. But in Boston, they say a Yankee is a Vermonter. What do Vermonters say about the whole business? Well, we know a Yankee is a farmer who eats pie for breakfast. And that's me. Breakfast without pie is as empty as a kiss without a hug. Especially in December.

Winter Notes

⚜

December morning melody
Makes music cold and slow.
My notes are footsteps, house to barn,
Written in the snow.

As I wrote early on, a
cow barn in winter is sure cozy. And in late December, there is a real Christmas meaning to the
place.

Manger Tale

⚜

A Christmas wind blows white and cold.
But in the barn,
The warmth of milk cows blankets me
Like woolen yarn.

August hay now whispers dry
In manger sweet,
Cattle lowly bend their heads
To gently eat.

The manger cradles bread of life
Down in its hole.
And with the hungry animals
I feed my soul.

In distant land so long ago
The tale was told.
And gifts were brought of frankincense,
Of myrrh and gold.

If worldly work shall make you need
A place for prayer,
Come shelter in my quiet barn.
A manger's there.

YOU know, I always thought that the First of January was a senseless time to start a new year. To me, it ought to annual on the First of April. Green and young instead of old and white.

Uproad from where we Pecks lived, there was an old man who went by the name of Early Pardee. As a lad I used to hunt rabbits with the old man. Most everybody in those parts used to predict that each winter was Early's last. Yet he lived on and on. With his white hair blowing, and his face as tough as the Rock of Ages, you could see Vermont in this man. Hands like hickory. His voice was soft, like the nighttime whisper of a February wind telling secrets to the rafters, a spike of frozen air.

Some said in town that there were those, his would-be heirs, who wanted him to die. But no one winter could fell a man like Early Pardee. It took a hundred.

An Old Man's Crust

⋈

The old man walks December's crust
Of snow. With each step light,
And carefully. Because he must
Not break into the white.

His gray December step is slow,
A calculating tread.
Before the April, we all know
The old man may be dead.

He'll never see another spring,
Another daffodil.
The churchbells possibly will ring
And crack the winter's still.

Yet on he walks, upon the cruel
December crust. Unstrong
Old man, intent that he may fool
Us all, and live on long.

THERE is a winter quiet
on a Vermont farm that can be enjoyed no place
else, as far as I know. Of course I haven't been
too many places, so I don't guess I'm qualified to
spout much. But when you walk in the wood

through snow dry as dust, hoping that by noon
the mercury might climb as high as zero, you
don't hear a sound. No birds, no rustle of leaves.
Only the hymn of snow packing under your
boots, like a dance to which you already know
the steps, even though your feet play a tune you
never yet heard.

So quiet. You start believing in the Benefactor
who created the silence in order to get your attention, to lightly tap your shoulder already hunched
over with the chill, and remind you to believe.

Then there is work to do, God's and yours:

Winter Worship

Not sickroom still, but often deathly pale;
A body growing cold in ten below.
Winter is a quiet white. Vermont,
Put to bed in coverlets of snow.

Through frosted window I can look the barn;
Silo full of corn, no longer green.
Tight against the barn it stands. Much like
The way against a church a spire leans.

What strange religious rite is there inside?
Religiously, twice daily I attend.
I do not hear a sermon, sing a hymn.
Instead to farmer's work my back I bend.

From rows of cows, as brown as wooden pews,
I take up my collection. There I squeeze
White kindly milk from each parishoner.
I work instead of pray there, on my knees.

I see a silent scripture in their tithe.
Although they do not give of gilt and gold,
They make me warm inside a milking barn.
Even when Vermont's December cold.

A certain hallowed happiness I find
Inside my barn and silo, like a kirk.
There is solemnity and peace for me.
My chapel is a barn. My prayer is work.

SOMETIMES what was
hurriedly written into fresh snow can get a soul
to thinking, about what he or she is, and what
does it all mean. Having work to do sure helps to
prod the answer. Work is a good poke in the ribs
for any conscience; more so, if you got somebody
to work for and to work with. Not always,
though. For work alone is a righteous prayer.

Farmers are tenders. As if knighted by the
Giver to look after what's down here on Earth
and to care for it best we can. Hard to say what
my religion is. Something to feel, but not something to smother with dogma.

Papa always said, "A man's faith counts for
naught, unless his dog and cat are the better for
it." I have a hunch Saul of Tarsus would nod to
that.

Rabbit Track

I was at a neighbor's farm,
Said goodbye and raised an arm
And started up the meadow hill,
Through a cold December still.

The heavens were a Quaker gray,
The snow was deep; boot high, I'd say.
I hunched my coat against my back,
And stepped across a rabbit track.

The wind had started to erase
His tracks. It cut across my face
To make me wonder—would it, too,
Wipe out my life when it was through?

There is never any doubt
What the world is all about—
Why we rise in morning dew,
Reaching for a workman's shoe.

Man was made to lift his head
From the patchwork of his bed
And tell his life, a simple yarn,
A pilgrimage out to his barn.

For himself and his, he'll fend.
His bread and wine are his to tend,
Be it grain or grape to feast
Upon, or be it land or beast . . .

To live's to tend, in my opinion.
God gave man this good dominion
To possess, to hold in deed,
Draw the water, drop the seed . . .

Close the blanket, watch it grow.
Battle with New England snow.
Keep the cellar fully binned.
Face the music of the wind.

Stand his ground with stubborn boots.
Hold his family name and roots
A sacred trust. Let nothing hide,
But speak his heritage with pride.

Know himself for what he be,
See himself as others see—
Just a tiller of the sod,
Who answers only unto God.

And what is my life worth? I know
It's just a rabbit track in snow.
At least a poet and a hare
Made tracks to say they went somewhere.

Death

TOOLS are necessary to
farming. And to a farmer. My father used to call
himself "a tired tool."

Try as I may, never could my hand seem to fit
the handle of a mallet or a saw or an axe the way
his hand could. Each tool seemed to be a part of
him, an extension of Haven Peck; almost as
though a knife handle was bone of his bone, like
Adam's rib. An axe would hitch his heart to the
heart of a felling tree; chip after chip, bite upon
bite, until the tree and the axe and the man were
all wed into one.

Tools

There upon the toolshed wall
I saw the pairs of pegs that he had sunk,
Each pair to snugly fit and choke
The neck of farming tools in rightly rows.

He's dead. My father, Haven Peck.
He died this morning sleeping in the barn.
And like his tools against this wall,
He must be put to rest in proper place.

Once buried, there'll be chores to do
To work this farm; as he had worked it, well.
And now that I am turned thirteen,
I'll try to be like him . . . a sharpened tool.

That's what he was, our Haven Peck,
A worn out tool to fit the hand of work
Just as the handles of a plow
Curve to rest beneath your fingertips.

Reaching for his shoeing tongs,
I took the wore-smooth handles in my hand.
The wood was gray with age, and yet
The gripping places yellow. Almost gold.

Basswood was my guess, because
It's soft enough to tunnel out a core
In which to drive the iron brace
Of handles; mean enough to purchase there.

Lean and tough, for basswood has
Such little weight. And yet the fibre in
Two basswood sleeves is firm enough to bite.
Resolute. So like his hands.

I saw my father work those tongs
And slowly pull a twisted horseshoe nail
From out a gentle foot. A mare
Whose hoof he cradled firm between his knees.

And while he worked he talked to her,
His Belgian mare who sweated as did he.
Horse and man together, tools.
He talked to her, to tell her not to fear.

His hands were busy, working tools
That needed full attention. But he rubbed
His head against the barrel of
Her side, to quiet her against the pain.

We bury him this afternoon.
Neighbors will be coming to the house.
We'll probable bring extra chairs
To the parlor from the kitchen table.

Two neighbors have already come.
I hear their hammers pounding pins in pine
To build a box for Haven Peck,
A man who died this morning in his barn.

And so beyond our orchard wall,
Among the rows of woodmarked graves of Pecks,
We'll rest him in his proper place.
I hung his tongs against the toolshed wall.

DEATH is the natural order of things; and some journeys of death, like the fall of an October leaf, have a final lustre all their own. Macbeth spoke of himself as the yellow leaf. Leaves in Vermont, just before they die, blast into blaring beauty.

The Last Waltz

October, October,
How red is your gown
As you gracefully waltz
With your coppery crown.

Foliage, Foliage
Dancing the hall
Of Autumn's grand ballroom,
Waltzing a fall.

Orchestra, Orchestra,
Wind in your hair,
Blowing your bugles
Of brass in the air.

November, November,
Blankets the floor.
The last waltz of crimson
Is waltzing no more.

THE death of a good
and faithful dog is close to being, in sorrow, like
the departure of a true friend. There is an im-
pending grief when I see an old man who lives
alone with an old dog. And how I hope that
when the times comes for one or the other, the
partner will join him in the journey, so they may
sort of help each other up that last flight of
risers.

The Needing

November snow had come and drifted. Almost
tumbled into windrows by an unseen
hayman. The land lay black and white
and warm, as one of spotted Holstein cows.

I was up upon the ridge, and looking
for spruce gum; clean and very good to chew.
Then I saw the old man and his burden,
across the dell and on the other ridge.

A dog he carried, stiff and cold as weather,
and a shovel. There he set them down
and rested on a rock. But not for long.
He upped himself, starting on his work.

The rocky land made the shovel ring.
It tolled upon the stone just like a churchbell.
Tolling for the dog perhaps. Stubborn land.
Yet surgeoned into by a stubborn man.

I walked closer, down then up. His face
was like the land in which he lived, Vermont.
Snow-capped, deep and furrowed; untillable.
He lifted rocky tumors from the earth.

Old and wrinkled as an empty purse.
Empty. Nothing in him left to spend
But yet he spent himself upon his work;
A widow's mite, and yet a manly might.

Carefully he lifted up the dog.
He gave his ear a stroking, one last time,
Making his deposit in the ground,
Tucking him inside the blanket soil.

Each by each, he piled the larger rocks
Atop the grave. A humble jagged cairn.
The work was done. But yet he did not rise.
He rested for a moment on his knees.

Below the ridge and through an alder patch,
I saw what must have been the old man's shack.
At least a quarter, maybe half a mile
away. Too far for such a deadened load.

Why had the old man borne the dog so far
To bury him upon a distant hill?
Perhaps the dog had needed this old man.
And after death, the climb prolonged the needing.

THERE is a line in the Holy Bible that I, as a most reverent observer of nature, could never accept. *Thou Shalt Not Kill.* Seems to me Our Lord never said anything like that. In fact, just the opposite; for in God's world, life is ordained to prey upon life. All living things are, in one way or another, predatory. There is something righteous to the manner in which a hawk earns his kill, his talons driving deep into the warm fur of a rabbit. He will then feed his mate and his young, and how could there be a higher calling?

Seems like every Christmas, I get a card from some well-meaning soul that pictures a lion lying down with a lamb. Sure, the two will lie together. One inside the other. Were I a lion, I would lie with a lioness. A whole pride of lionesses. But please, not with a lamb.

Cat and Mouse

It is the law. Our cat has caught a mouse.
Across the field she trots with squealing booty.
She'll bring him up the walk; and to the house.
To show us, I suspect, she does her duty.

Lightly in her mouth she holds his head.
A mouse near death, and with a pounding heart
He knows his time is come. He'll soon be dead.
His warm gray body will be torn apart.

I could scold her for her hunting act
And take away the mouse that she has caught
To set him free again in distant tract
And feed her from a can of food I bought.

I will not disobey the law. I learn
How wrong it is to take what others earn.

I NEVER had a sister Priscilla.
But a boyhood friend of mine did. And when
she died at the early age of seven years, I wanted
to hurt inside as much as I knew my pal Soup,
her brother, was hurting. So I imagined that
Soup's sister was my sister . . .

A Sister's Grave

The grave was three feet long, or less. More like
A well than grave, and deeper down than wide.
It only took one man with lowering ropes
To let her coffin drop itself inside.

Pneumonia, they said. I did not know
Just what that was. A something beyond belief.
Our family stood all dressed in Sunday black.
As I held Papa's hand it shook with grief.

Bits of earth, fresh, clinging to our shoes,
Beside her grave we stood, as at her bed
We earlier had stood, not knowing then
Nor now why she was dying, why she's dead.

Eight in June, my sister would have been
If she had lived. A story just begun.
Her hair, how brown it was. With just some red
Enough inside the curls to trap the sun.

I'd picked a daisy, taken it to her
Up to her room. And tried to give it to her.
Her hands were still and open on the quilt.
I touched them with the stem. They did not stir.

To and fro I teased the daisy stem
Upon her arm, to tickle her awake.
But she was not asleep. And yet, asleep.
Nor any notice of me did she make.

"Priscilla," I had said to her at last,
"Priscilla, can't you hear me? Please wake up.
If you do you get a daisy. See?
And then I'll bring a yellow buttercup."

Mama came, her apron wiping hands
That were not wet. She'd started doing that:
Going to her apron with her hands,
Even in the evening when she sat.

"Robert," Mama said, "your sister's dead.
Get Papa from the barn. Please hurry. Go."
I ran along, in dream, out to the barn.
Papa came. "She's dead." He said, "I know."

Down it went; her coffin, handleless.
A coffin quickly cut, unpainted wood.
I looked upon it. As it dropped below,
How I hated it from where I stood.

The earth was spaded in. Each shovelful
Would drum the lid, each getting softer. And
It was done. We could not walk away.
We could not leave a patch of grassless land.

WHEN I was a kid,
Soup and I and a few more of us boys had a pal
who was a man with white hair. He sort of
looked the way somebody's grandpa should look,
but none of us were his grandchildren.
Yet we sure were his pals:

To Catlin

We called him Mr. Catlin. He was old,
And we were boys, and half as tall to him.
His shack stood at the end of gravel road,
But freshly painted yellow, sides and trim.

Before the turn of road brought shack to view,
A nose could tell its presence by the smell
Of woodsmoke from his old black cooking stove.
Inside, the smoking said, were tales to tell.

That old black stove knew flapjack batter well.
Without a griddle, Catlin poured out spots
Of yellow batter, bubbling as they fried.
We ate the pancakes, butterless and hot.

Against a wall a single wooden cot
On which an Army blanket always lay.
There sat Catlin; fiddle on his knee,
Not under chin. We'd beg to hear him play.

Square-dance music, that was what he knew.
Tunes that hit the ear, but did not stop
Inside the ear, but sank into the toes
To fester there and cause our feet to hop.

Corncobs dried for pipes behind a chair
Once painted black. The arms were worn to tan—
Smooth from hands that held them; and to boot,
Held a conversation, man to man.

He knew baseball. Baseball stories, too—
About the one Ty Cobb. He'd seen him play.
And horses. He had seen the great Dan Patch
Win a heat, when he had bet the bay.

Catlin played harmonica besides.
You'd never believe one man could know the list
Of songs he knew. I'd like to hum one now,
To tell our Mr. Catlin how he's missed.

MR. CATLIN was some gent. Never once did he swear, or say a sorry word about a neighbor. I liked him best when he'd try to clog dance and play the harmonica all at once. He'd get all out of breath, and we'd all get to laughing at him. Mr. Catlin would laugh, too.

He lived alone; and every once in a blue moon, his breath wouldn't smell like flapjacks and coffee, and instead he'd smell sort of strange. That's when there would be an empty bottle. But I guess he was lonely after his wife died.

The name of Mr. Catlin's horse was Dobbin, and there wasn't a horse in all Vermont that got as much kindness as she did. I felt real bad when he sold her. So did Soup.

Not too long ago, I got to thinking about the death of a man I didn't know. Fact is, I never even knew the fellow's name. I just sort of started to wonder who he was and this is how it come about:

North Fence

My north stonefence is down. It begs my tend.
Some stones have tumbled loose to cut a U
For restless Holstein cows to wander through
Into my neighbor's corn, unless I mend.

My cows, his corn; an oil and water mix.
And so to keep him his and me my own,
It's time to scrape my fingers, put the stone
Back into place and pay my fence a fix.

Winter snow can sit the fence's top
And melt to water pockets, once more freeze
And move big boulders, easy as you please,
That I cannot. And join a cow to crop.

The fence is straight, an honest perfect line;
Built by hands long dead and layed away.
But yet his fence is lingering today
Between my neighbor's property and mine.

At first the land was his, to feel his plow
Push its virgin bite and open up
To take his seed, like woman, give him sup.
Perhaps he rests nearby. It owns him, now.

Taken him inside its body, deep;
That first freeholder, who had piled this wall
And watched his neighbor's foddercorn grow tall.
Taken him to earthly breast, to keep.

My neighbor sees me work. He walks his hoe
Up to the wall dividing his and mine
To help me lift a stone, and pass the time
Of day. But then he says he'd best to go.

A tribulation, fitting fencing stones
Into their former places. As they were
When they were first put there. Then set astir.
My muscle ache drives deep into my bones.

Why is it that I always have so much
Of stone left over when my patching's done?
I try to fit them back right, each to one;
But never do. How cold they are to touch.

Cold, and like the man who made the start
Of my north fence a century ago—
To separate a cow from cornfield, so.
A fence sets men together, not apart.

YEARS before I wrote *A Day No Pigs Would Die*, I got to thinking on a pet pig that I raised up, back in the days when I was getting raised up myself. Her name was Pinky. And because of her, and my father, I learned early the meaning of what it was to be a man. And by means of a pig's death, what my life was all about:

Manhood

⚜

April had come to Vermont with a shout,
Shaking its coverlets, rousting it out,
Popping its greenery, budding each twig.
To raise, I got given a tiny white pig.

Her first night alone, I'd slept in the barn.
Colder than Blitzen. Did I give a darn?
We snuggled together, the pig near my face,
So she wouldn't feel lonely and strange in the
    place.

Pinky, I named her. Because of her nose
And her ears, and the color between her two toes.
She squealed once or twice with me, during the
    night.
In a mountain of blankets we cuddled up tight.

May month and June month, how Pinky ate
The sweet milky mash. And she added on weight.
When the hot of July brought the first foddercorn,
You'd think she'd been starved since the day
   she was born.

August, September, and was she a pig!
I was so proud that she grew up so big
That we took her to Rutland, September the first.
When she took a ribbon, I thought I would burst.

Winning a ribbon at Rutland State Fair
is no easy matter. I know. I was there,
And those judges who looked at her don't miss a
   thing.
But she took a ribbon. I wanted to sing!

October felled acorns and Pinky loved those.
She'd root under butternut trees with her nose—
And paw at the leaves. Pinky would hunt
Til she found what she looked for, giving a grunt.

The weather went colder. November came 'round,
And like Mama's cakeboard, it floured the ground
With a coating of snow. It said winter was soon.
The sky in the evening was missing a moon.

The days of November were deepening gray.
Closer and closer and closer the day
That I knew would arrive. How I hated our clock.
Each tick made the knowing as heavy as rock.

I dreaded the winter, hating the fall.
Hating November, hating it all.
Remembering April, remembering how
My Pinky had grown from a piglet to sow.

Colder and colder, the weather contrived.
A Saturday came. The day had arrived.
Breakfast was silent, and nobody spoke.
Papa fingered his pipe, but he just couldn't smoke.

I knew its meaning. The end of a life.
Papa then sharpening the pig-sticking knife.
He handed it to me. Its long silver blade
Shook in my fingers like it was afraid.

We went to the pig pen, just Papa and me.
Papa had said, "What must be, it must be."
But something within me was hollering, "No!"
So Papa then emptied her blood on the snow.

April is laughter, and April brings toys.
But sober November makes men out of boys.
Then Papa spoke to me. "Manhood, my son—
Manhood is doing what has to be done."

Hard Work

KILLING hogs, or writing a poem; both professions of dignity . . . yet no matter what you do, hard work will make you do it better.

If you must, call yourself a writer. But you're a simpleton if you tarry around expecting the sweet Muses to drop down from heaven to kiss you lightly on the brow with inspiration. Writing is not an art. Writing is a *craft*, like making a good saddle.

Suppose I hand you a sheet of raw leather and said, "Make me a saddle." What would your first saddle look like?

Chances are it wouldn't be fit to sit, and you'd probable get a questioning look from the first mare you threw your first saddle on. But your third saddle, and your tenth saddle, and your thirty-first? Keep working, you'll get the hang of it. An idle pen is sorry as an idle hoe. So I debt up much of my success to all my Vermont folk who made me work.

You could say that hard work is the icon of Vermont. Work is respected more than money or charm. We needed a mortgage on our farm one time, to meet some payments and settle some accounts. Papa made his mark, his X, on the paper and Banker Rockwood put the dollars in Papa's hand. Just like that.

"You're a worker, Haven."

That was all that was said, as it was more a bond of trust than a business transaction. Backbone collateral, signed in sweat. As a boy, I witnessed the exchange, and felt proud that people trusted my father to such a degree. The loan was paid off. Not one soul in the county dared to doubt that it would be. Loans were made and debts were paid, and that's all there was to this code of simple security.

Our town statue said it all:

The Granite Sentry

Up in Vermont, an old old town
Surrounds a village square.
A granite sentry leans upon
His granite musket there.

The barns are red, the houses white,
A brook runs to a pool.
And underneath a bridge, a jug
Of cider keeps its cool.

Green hills are paletted with hues
Of maple trees that tap,
And sugar houses sweeten brown
With age and smoking sap.

Working days are long and lean
On rough and rocky tracts.
Precious little idle talk,
And fewer idle backs.

Yankee muscle reaps the stone
To wall the fields with fence.
Yankee dollars, Yankee banks
Entrusting Yankee sense.

Sober hymns on Sunday morn
Are sung by solid folk,
Born and raised to interlock
As beams of solid oak.

The soldier stands, a guardian
To keep the peace and prayer.
The granite sentry leans upon
His granite musket there.

ALTHOUGH my father (and all the men in the vicinity) relied on hard work to earn our bread, there was often a softness in his manner. In church, his big hands held a hymnal as if to bless it with the strength of his touch.

The Carpenter of Nazareth sought out the company of *working men.* Not the Sadducee or the Pharisee in their robes of silk; but instead, a band of Galilee fishers who probable brawled like the wharf rats on the docks of any waterfront, sang bawdy ballads, and no doubt engaged in some jolly good wenching. I can see the hands of Jesus, thick with work, and even powdered yellow with the sawdust of fresh timbers. I am thankful He came as a carpenter and not as a poet.

Hymn

The congregation rumbles to its feet.
Big tired feet of farmers, side by side.
Clumsy fingers find the page, to meet
The good and holy verses there inside.

Once the hymnals were a shining new.
But now they're old, and worn out to the touch.
And many hands that lift them from the pew
To hold them—they are old and worn as much.

[67]

They stand, when first the melody takes flight.
A flowered organist gives all a nod.
Lungs fill deep and leather throats unite
To sing "A Mighty Fortress Is Our God."

They say in song, with voices rough as weather:
Men cannot quarrel once they sing together.

MY good mother always said that there was little wrong with this world that *sweat* couldn't wash away.

Mama and Aunt Carrie are still alive as I write this page. Still working, and believing in the righteousness of the tasks they perform and a job well turned. They are small ladies, both weigh less than a hundred-pound sack of sorghum. Resolute women. Mama is now eighty-six and Aunt Carrie is ninety-one. My aunt had to go to the hospital recently for an overnight checkup. The night nurse said, "I'll take your teeth," thinking they were false.

"Huh," said Aunt Carrie, "you'll need tongs to do it."

Hard work, years upon seasons and days after decades of it, has packed both women into a mold near firm as marble. The two of them sort of go together like the beams of an old barn.

To Leather

Wool is winter; Cotton, spring.
Satin is a ball
To dance with Silk in fancy fling,
A waltz throughout the hall.

Linen sings a hymnal stern
And at the table blesses.
Taffeta is quick to learn
An awkward boy's caresses.

Gingham bakes an apple pie
And goes to picnics, too.
Lyle runs down from pretty thigh
Into a dainty shoe.

But hallowed is the hide of cow
That boots the farmer's feet.
It aprons smith at forge, and how
It scorches black with heat.

Leather harnesses the soil
And halters up a bull;
Trudges fields of burning toil,
A stubborn plow to pull.

Frilly Frock will never do
The job Old Leather can.
It works until the day is through
And knows the sweat of man.

WHEN I was a boy, it always seemed that we lads were required to work every minute. There's an old story, maybe from Vermont and maybe not, that probable got writ by a working man whose misfortune it was to have a mess of boys as his helpmates. The man said:

> One boy is worth one boy.
> Two boys are half a boy.
> Three boys are no boy at all.

I got a hunch the farmer who wrote that trio of thoughts had Soup and me plus my cousin, Ben Peck, for half-growed helpers.

To earn a few dollars one summer, I'd hired myself out (at the age of twelve) to a neighboring farmer to help him string a fence. His name was Tanner, and he wasn't known for smiling a whole lot. At least not every decade. Long about noon on my first day, Papa planned his work to be close on to ours, so he hoofed over to see how I was faring. He arrived on the scene just as I'd twisted out a fresh post-hold (you cross your hands first, in order to give the handle a double lick). When I sunk the post it was as crooked as a mayor's smile.

Mr. Tanner took one look at the sorry lean of the post, a second look at me, then a third at Papa. "Haven Peck," he said to my father, "you're a good neighbor. But you're a damn poor sire."

Ben Peck, who was my age and a third cousin, and I were the two worst tomfools in Vermont when it come to doing anything other than work. We could go miles out of our way to duck a chore, and think up some fancy excuses if the work was too nearby to run away from:

On Relief

One afternoon, my cousin Ben
and I were rassling in the hay
up in the loft. We stopped to wipe
the hayseed off our necks and rest.

All was quiet. Then we noticed
Mr. Caleb Stoner come
across the field and speak to Papa
in the barn, just underneath.

Mr. Stoner did the talking,
Papa mostly listening;
as Ben and I were unbeknown
to Mr. Stoner and to Papa.

"He don't work," said Mr. Stoner,
"not no more. He's on relief."
"On relief?" repeated Papa.
"On relief," said Leb again.

"I tell you," said Mr. Stoner,
"George T. Cassman is a drone,
a low down good-for-nothing man."
"Able-bodied, too," said Papa.

"Seven children George begot
himself," said Caleb. "Now you'd think
responsibility would prick
a spur into his lazy ribs.

"But no! Not George T. Cassman.
Brother, he is on relief to stay,
I'll wager. On relief to stay,
Some claim he'll never work again."

"You don't say," said Papa now
to Caleb Stoner. Then he lit
his pipe again while Mr. Stoner
talked of Mr. Cassman more.

"The man is getting on, I reckon,
Like the rest of us good folks.
But George T. Cassman is a year
or two the younger side of me."

"On relief," said Papa, leaning
one foot on the manger bin,
elbow to his knee. And Mr.
Stoner said, "A crying shame!

"Driving, I was, by his place
this morning. Fences broken down
and missing slats. The cow barn roof
needs patching. Bet it leaks like Hell."

"Do tell," said Papa, rocking back
and forth upon his standing leg,
"do tell." So Mr. Caleb Stoner
told and told and told and told.

"Imagine that!" said Mr. Stoner,
finger-pointing Papa's chest.
"I sometimes wonder what the world
is coming to." And Papa nodded.

Later, Mama collared Ben
and put him thinning out the dill.
And Papa got me started, after,
shoring up the apple branches.

I was tuckered out from rassling
Ben; and in the apple orchard,
it was shady. And the grove was
a piece away from Papa's work.

Lying down beneath an apple
tree, I took a bite or two
of Jonathan. Before I knew it,
I was sleeping long and gone.

"Robert!" I heard Papa's voice;
and it was thunder, I tell you.
My eyes were open, looking up
at him. He stood right at my feet.

"You sick?" asked Papa. "No," I said,
"I'm on relief, like Mr. Cassman."
"Oh, you're on relief," said Papa.
A willow spear was in his hand.

"It may be you're on relief,"
said Papa, "but this switch is not."
Before it cut me 'cross the knees,
I was shoring apple trees.

MY father usually had little to say about the able-bodied who didn't work, and wanted to feed off the sweat of neighbors. But you can bet that what he thought of such lazy louts wouldn't be righteous to repeat. When our downroad neighbor, George Cassman, worked too little and begot too often (seven children, same as us Pecks) Papa and I would ride our wagon past the Cassman place and my father would just shake his head. Their farm was idle land. Papa never spoke on it. Yet I felt his resent of a man who'd bring children into the world for other men to bend their backs to support.

Papa never give words to it, as he just wasn't the kind of man who'd flail a neighbor.

If that Cassman fellow was the most shiftless soul in town, one of the hard-working was Mr. Chaplow, our blacksmith. He was not a big man, but average in height, and lean as a bean. Not a gram of fat on him. Barehanded he could spread a horseshoe, probably because the iron was still hot. So hot that not another man in the county could barehand it. With his fingers, he could pick up a redhot coal from the forge bed and juggle it so fast that it wouldn't burn him. His given name was Interest.

Sometimes I'd dream of dying and going to Hell, and who'd always be there in the red-hot embers? Interest Chaplow. Being a smith, especially on a hot July day, sure is a devil's work.

No mortal man could eat all that heat. You'd think Mr. Chaplow would've had a hot temper to match his work, but no. His voice was soft as a vesper. Behind his smithy, on the south side, he grew yellow roses.

Mr. Chaplow and Papa agreed on one facet of blacksmithing, and it was this: "Always shoe hot," Papa said to me, "and never trust a man who shoes cold."

Reckon there's a reason. A mare is like a woman. She wants to put her hoofs in warm slippers.

Shoeing Up the Mare

Winter's long,
But Spring is song
When swallows flute the air.
Hornets hum.
The time is come
For shoeing up the mare.

From earth unfirm
A fishing worm
Is pulled by robin red.
Frisky heels
Kick daisy fields
And rub against the shed.

The road to town
Is muddy brown
But Betsy steps out light.
Reins hang loose
For it's no use
To try to hold her tight.

The hammer's peal
Upon the steel
Sends sparks up to the roof.
Up with ease
Between his knees
The smith holds Betsy's hoof.

Once in hand
The iron band
Is pounded to the core.
One by one
The job gets done
And Betsy raps the floor.

Trotting home
The fields of loam
Are green with gifts of God.
Everything
Is really spring
When we get Betsy shod.

Sun Dance

Happy as a whistle.

That was sort of the way all us folks felt when old white winter ran downhill and jumped into the crick, and was replaced by a new green spring.

Papa always made me a whistle, every April, or sometimes early May. Sumac works well, but basswood or poplar are also good whistle wood.

Sumac Whistle

April's here, to cut for me
A whistle. Find a sumac tree
Out beyond the creek that's lean,
I'd say finger-thick, and green.

Search a section near a crotch
To punch a blowhole. Cut a notch
Like so. Then it should be a cinch
To slip the bark sleeve half an inch.

Bucket soak it overnight
So the bond gets locked on tight
Enough to hold. It's smooth and round
To blow a sumac whistle sound.

Draw a breath that's full and deep
Or you won't produce a peep
Of a yellow chick. That's right,
Put it to your mouth real tight.

And blow! With all your might and main.
You'll stab some poor soul's ear a pain.
And jump? He'll leave his shoes beneath
His feet. Or maybe pop his teeth.

You won't make friends but enemies
For yourself and sumac trees
But there's no sweeter April toy—
A sumac whistle for a boy.

EVER build yourself a
flutter wheel? Some boys call 'em flutter mills.
Same thing. Little riverlets of spring seemed almost to whimper for a wheel to turn, like a kid
who wants a friend to frolic with. When I was a
lad, no April ever went without.

One boy and one tiny stream were good for a
whole afternoon, when it was still too muddy for
baseball and too early for the brook trout to bite.
There's a magic in water that pulls at all man-
kind and womankind; I guess because we were
once water creatures ourselves, years back, and
we still hanker to home back to where we spawn.

Maybe we cotton to water because it is so
childlike. As it runs, it laughs.

Flutter Wheel

April sun awakes the sleeping land,
As if to rouse it up from deep below
The layers of whitely quilts of winter. And
to wash its drowsy face with melting snow.

Riverlets, the springtime's morning tears,
Are spilling down the mountain cheeks to fill
The pond. It's time! The winter skies are clear
For summer. I've a flutter wheel to build.

A narrow but a constant stream I spy
To turn my mill. My pocketknife will cut
A brace of tiny crotches, inches high.
And then a basswood axle for a strut.

Birchbark blades that number four will fit
To form the paddles of the wheel. On them,
One sharp end to jam into a slit
Or two I cut into the axle stem.

Before the flutter wheel can turn, I place
A dab of mud into each crotch, to ease
The friction where the axle tips will case.
And thus it spins! As willing as you please.

Around it goes. Each blade is swiftly sent
By mountain stream. Why don't you come and look,
And watch it as it works in gay content?
A flutter wheel that turns an April brook.

SAD enough that so many folks never built a flutter wheel in April, and the same number of deprived persons never whipped an apple.

Took little strength, no imagination, and even less brains . . . so you can see quick off that it was the perfect pastime for Luther Wesley Vinson and Robert Newton Peck (Soup and me). You hold the tiny and very hard apple close to your chest, pushing the pointed stick into the green skin. Then your whip was loaded and ready to let go. Try it sometime. You'll be awed at the distance you can scat an apple. If the whip is long enough, and the apple weight just right, that little greening will sail out of sight. Well, near to.

Sure was fun. Soup and Ben Peck and I whipped enough apples for a million pies. Well, at least a thousand.

Mama and Aunt Carrie said that we were to always skin off our shirts. But we were too busy to wait. And so when the pointed stick bit the apple, the juice would spurt all over a shirtfront. Apple stain wouldn't wash out. It stuck like a brother.

Whipping Apples

In July, the apples on
The meadow tree were small
And green and hard as marbles,
And bittersweet as gall.

Out of question, eating one;
Although we'd often try.
But we could send one flying
Almost clean across the sky.

From the marsh we'd cut a long
And whippy willow stick.
We'd sharp one end. The handle end
was trigger-finger thick.

On the pointed end we'd push
An apple greening, so.
Then we'd take a windup whip,
And then we'd let her go!

The stick would whistle through the air,
The apple would take flight.
If you got a good one
It would sail right out of sight.

But distance wasn't just the goal;
We'd often aim as well,
And try to hit the tower
And the Baptist Church's bell.

We knew we shouldn't do it.
We'd been told that it was wrong.
But it was sport to make an apple
Hit that golden gong.

Mama knew we'd done it,
And to fib was just no use.
Because our shirts were spotted brown
With drops of apple juice.

With fondness I remember
Doing that when 'ere I see
A marsh of whippy willows
And a greening apple tree.

YOU don't have to tell a
kid where a sump hole is. Come a hot day, he'll
seek it. Ours was about a mile off, in a place
called the Burly Lot; an old quarry that got used
sometimes, and sometimes just lay fallow.
Mothers hated it. Soup would whisper "Burly
Lot" into my ear as a destiny, and of course I'd
yell out "*Burly Lot*" and get Mama's or Aunt
Carrie's denial. Soup would look my way and
sigh.

I was never allowed to set foot in the Burly
Lot and neither was Soup. We went often.

You could fall off the high rocky cliffs and
then half drown in the sump water that filled the

basin down below. It was the best place in the world to go. Soup and I never went anywhere unless we'd first exhausted all chances of getting to the Burly Lot for several hours of deviltry.

The rock-workers had an old shack over there, which was reputed to still hold dynamite. I spent hours, days, weeks, years . . . trying to break into that abandoned shack, just to see what a stick of genuine dynamite looked like. So did Soup. But we never got inside, lucky for us.

Everybody I knew tried to get into the shack and thought it was truly a worthy project; except for Mama or Aunt Carrie or Mrs. Vinson or somebody like that. Well, even though the interior of the dynamite shack is still a mystery in my mind, the Burly Lot sure was a place to go in hot weather:

Summer Sump

Summer's oven bids the corn
To rise, as if to bake as bread.
To serve the sun high on its throne,
Pronouncing that the wind is dead.

Obediently aspens lower
Their heads as worshippers. It's June—
When only bugs and boys disturb
The solemn mass of afternoon.

Barefoot, jumping windrows to
The sump, the young snakes shed their skins,
Dip a dusty toe, and hiss
"It's cold!" And bravely slither in.

Bracken curtains mask the stage
Where naked players, acting out
Their parts as large white frogs, all
Kicking legs. Each line they shout.

Savor every drop. For soon
We soak our heads beneath the pump.
Because there is no swimming when
Cruel August drains away the sump.

WE boys never wore a swimsuit. And the worst thing in the whole world was to trudge all the way over to the Burly Lot, only to find *girls* (who *always* wore bathing suits) in the sump hole. One day was so hot we went in anyhow (naked as jaybirds) and all the girls screamed. Then they sort of got used to the idea and nobody, clad or unclad, seemed to be too bothered about it. Except during the diving. We backed in.

Summer began with a bang!
The nearest town to our farm had a population around two thousand people, yet a greater

number of Holstein cows; and the big event of warm weather was the Four of July. Sure was a heck of a long day. Seems like by the time I got home to bed after the fireworks, I'd already:

1. cried
2. throwed up
3. ripped my trousers

Usually all three; or at least, several interesting combinations.

The Four of July parade was always early in the morning, before it got so hot that the tuba player couldn't blast Weed Hill. The tubist, Willis Foley, was really a clerk in Holton's Hardware Store. And the tuba was really a Sousaphone, big as a churchbell, silver on the outside, brassy inside the horn. To make matters worse, Weed Hill was steep in places, and Willis was a small man. But no one else could play it, so poor Willis blasted away, *poom* after *poom*, all the way along Main Street and up Weed Hill to where the monument of the sentry was. The granite sentry was a Minuteman, and as it was the Four of July, the parade seemed destined to get that far, due to determination and pangs of patriotism.

At the end of each march (up at the monument) Willis Foley announced every year that this was his last parade. "I ain't getting any younger, and that dang Weed Hill ain't growing any shorter."

Yet year after year, Willis bore his brassy burden, note after note, and step after step, until finally someone suggested that the parade *start* up at the Sentry and march *downhill* instead of up. Everyone was elated, as it was (to use a Four of July term) rather revolutionary and in keeping with a rebellious tradition. Everybody agreed, except for Willis.

"We never went that way before," he said. Willis has seen plenty of changes come to our town, and was proud to announce how he'd opposed every one of 'em:

Four of July

Into my trousers before it was dawn,
With nary a bother to give a good yawn.
Down into breakfast the family got.
Papa said, "Mother, it's going to be hot."

We hitched up the mare and we buckled her
    down,
Piled in the buggy and headed for town.
We got to a spot that was covered with shade.
Somebody shouted, "Here comes the parade!"

Purple and orange and yellow balloons,
Trumpets and trombones and contra-bassoons.
Tubas and clarinets, bass drum and snare
Blasted a Sousa march, filling the air.

Volunteer Firemen, old Number One
Was so shiny and red as it rolled in the sun.
The American Legion, Police officers blue,
The National Guard with a casson or two.

An old Gold-Star Mother who gave up her boy.
Red firecrackers exploding with joy.
Yelling and cheering and laughing and fun.
Afternoon baseball, the old home team won.

Potato sack races and kites on the fly,
A pie-eating contest with blueberry pie.
Baskets of picnics laid out in the park,
Awaiting the fireworks when it got dark.

Skyrockets wounding the heaven we saw,
Gasping the wonder and bursting with awe,
Standing stock still in the crowd and its stare
As white Roman candles would sparkle the air.

That beautiful day was so wonderful big,
That I slept the way home in the back of the rig,
And dreamed of Old Glory against a blue sky.
God surely hallowed the Four of July.

JUST like our sump hole, the one we swam in over in the Burly Lot, we also had a creek (we said *crick*) that ran its own seasons, flood to dry.

The Crick was one of the social spots when I was a lad. It wasn't very deep, and so the town mothers usually didn't work up too wet a worry. Except near the Dam. We were told, maternal fingers in our faces, that never were we to go near the Dam. But in late August or early September, our village creek was so low that its bed was green with summer moss.

Now when the water got so scarce that it wasn't fit even to wade in, we looked for a deeper wet. Just above the Dam. The Dam was a place, like the movies or the Burly Lot, or the monument of our Sentry. When either Soup or I talked about the Dam, it was just a place to swim. But when Soup's mother or my mother talked about the Dam, it always sounded like they were swearing.

"That old *Dam*," my mother would say to Aunt Carrie. And then my aunt would agree, allowing that to her mind the town ought to fence it off. Thank the good jolly nobody ever did. The water in the Dam was thirty foot deep, and you weren't anybody until you could dive all the way to the bottom and bring up a fistful of gravel as proof.

September Creek

By end of March, the cold will ease.
A winter snow begins to thaw
In circles brown. How like a cheese,
The sun bores holes of tired straw.

High above are northbound geese.
I do not yet hear robbins sing.
The sheep are climbing in their fleece
Up land determined to be Spring.

All summer long the creek is high,
Rushing to its destiny.
Until the August swallows dry,
The bottom of its glass to see.

Lazy creekbed rocks are round.
They lie in bed, their bellies green
With summer moss. Just halfly gowned.
A wren will light on one to preen.

A willow freckles next year's bud,
And as a sentry stands alone.
An auto tire lies in mud.
Some thoughtless dolt in there has thrown.

It makes my collar hot to look.
Humanity has loathly freaks
To carelessly defile a brook.
A shame they don't dry up. Like creeks.

THE last gasp of summer come in September, marked by our annual pilgrimage to Rutland Fair.

I never did go until I was twelve, and the first time I saw Rutland Fair I said to myself . . . this is it. This is the place. I don't want to ever be anywhere but right here at the Fair Grounds.

Sure enough, most everyone thought the same thought, because just about everyone attended the state fair. And there was something for everyone. Quilts to pickles to pies for Mama and Aunt Carrie. Papa always wanted to be a judge for the pie contest, as the judges got to eat all they wanted of all the pie their insides could hold. Must have been near to Paradise. But pie was only one thing out of a hundred things that got judged. Every good that you'd canned or put-by for winter got itself valued; which brought a few tears to the eyes of more than one country woman whose rhubarb conserve got a blue ribbon.

My mother made the best rhubarb conserve. Not just in Vermont, but in the whole world. And I'd admit that the best angelfood cake was made by Aunt Carrie. Light as laughter. And whiter than a Sunday snow. Aunt Carrie said that the secret was to use brown eggs because more white went into the egg of a brown egg, instead of getting used up on a white shell.

Make sense to you? Well, it would if'n you'd bite her cake.

Trotters or pacers? That was an age old question on the subject of which horse could sing a sulky faster around the track, and there wasn't one farmer in Vermont who didn't take a stance on the matter, with a theory behind it. Rutland Fair had eight races a day, so there was ample exposure of horse speed to figure it all out.

Our neighbor's pacer was Gray Lady and after one heat (one race) I got given the lead rope and was allowed to walk her cool for an hour, so she wouldn't stiffen up. Whenever a person looked poorly, somebody would always josh him to say: "You look like you been rode hard and put away wet."

Rutland Fair

I've never been to Heaven
But I guess I know what's there.
I figure Heaven's got to be
Just like a Rutland Fair.

September never ever gets
Here soon enough. I say
I count the days until we go
To Rutland for the day.

We take Mars, our Holstein bull,
And lead him by his nose
Into the ring. He earns a ribbon
Every time he shows.

The year that Mama's pickles won
I thought she'd almost cry.
Aunt Carrie won the tasting
With her huckleberry pie.

The oxen pulling contest's where
Excitement is. I'll boast
That Uncle Micah's Cicero
And Caesar move the most.

They piled on stones a plenty high
For Micah's team to draw.
They moved it on the final try
Without a gee or haw.

Our neighbor's pacer took two heats.
But almost lost the race
When that bay gelding up from Cornwall
Gave her goodly chase.

I got given ten whole cents,
And then a nickel found.
I rode the ferris wheel and swings
And merry-go-around.

Before I went to sleep that night
I knelt and said a prayer
For empty-hearted folks who never
Been to Rutland Fair.

Critters

WHAT'S a critter?

Well, I don't guess it could mean much more than a slang word for creature. I suppose, though, you knew that in some parts of Vermont, years back, folks called corn fritters by the name of corn features.

To me, a critter is any form of life that's neither a vegetable nor a human. Also applies to a mean man. But a critter that becomes pesky is a varmit. Yet if it can be trapped or gunned to stuff in the stew pot, then the varmit becomes a vittle, which is also a corn fritter, which rhymes with critter. So as you can see, we come clear around the barn to chase our own tail.

When I was logging for the papermill, our lumber camp had a critter that got to be a varmit. I'd sort of been lay-wait to catch him for near to a week:

The Cornering

The lumber camp was quiet. It was noon.
Black dinner pails sat open, resting on
a tablecloth of golden yellow chips;
many with a heart of deeper brown.

We ate and dozed. Asleep but not asleep.
A noise disturbed us from a nearby shed.
"There's that weasel," someone softly said.
We heard the rattle of an empty can.

I put on two thick pairs of working gloves.
Quietly I sneaked up on the shed,
and to the door, intent to capture him.
On hands and knees, I slowly crept inside.

How small he was! A coat of reddish brown;
his underside was yellow, near to white.
Front paws against his chest, he hissed at me.
The tiny ears went flat against his head.

I had him cornered, blocking his escape.
Now I held the center of the room.
He was only ten short feet away.
His mouth was wide, to bare his ring of fangs.

With his speed, he could have skirted me
on either side, and said a quick goodbye.
But no, not he! It hardly crossed his mind.
Instead he made his lunge right to my throat.

[99]

In the next two seconds, I can swear
that I was bitten eighty-seven times.
I never knew what hit me when he charged.
He felt like forty weasels, not just one.

As fast as he had come, he took his leave;
I confess I did not see him go.
But great was my relief at his farewell,
glad his want was not to capture me.

Other weasels I have met in life.
Weasels tall as I, and taller yet.
I've been careful not to corner them,
but always give them avenue around.

No one, be he animal or man,
appreciates a corner at his back.
A weasel, cornered, can be stubborn stuff.
And four thick gloves are often not enough.

MY mother once had a
wild gray squirrel so tame that it would enter our
kitchen and scold her until she rustled up some
seeds for a snack. This is rare. Usually when
squirrels are this tame, it's because they tumbled
from their nest and were nursed and fondled by
human hands instead of maternal paws. Mama's
squirrel was wild, except with her. No one else,
with the one exception of Aunt Carrie, could
come close.

Mama used to pick wild mushrooms to give
her pet a special treat.

Mushrooms

Little lowly people of the earth
Who live unseen beneath the buried brown,
Will show their heads, a small community;
And bicker in their crowded little town.

A colony, all leghorn white and smooth,
Make appearance on a single day;
And raise their children all about as chicks.
Up they grow, and then to move away.

One mushroom boy has freckles on his face.
His gangled legs will wobble in the dew
As if to say he does not care to dance
At all, despite his party suit is new.

Across the leafy ballroom, nests of girls
Await, all gowned in crimson, yellow, green—
Heads together, whispering of him;
Each one hoping that she will be seen.

The party is disrupted when a squirrel
Appears, to nibble at a mushroom treat.
His tiny paws reach out to break a piece
From off the edge, to turn it; then to eat.

The squirrel sees me, but does not scamper off.
Perhaps he knows he need not be too shy.
We mushroom fanciers are gentle folk.
We come to visit mushrooms, squirrel and I.

As I have always been a wild mushroom fancier, a friend of mine (who is rather a wit) has suggested a title for my *last* book:

"Eating the Wild Mushroom"
by the *late* R.N. Peck

Needless to say, one bite of a toadstool and life is over. Toadstools, which look so much like mushrooms it's spooky, are deadly poison. So you best take heed, you and your squirrel. Never heard of a squirrel dying from toadstool poisoning, so maybe they're brighter than all the humans who bit a toadstool and then bit the dust. All to the good, I reckon.

On a farm, death is ever at hand.

I guess because I have personally butchered so many critters, I am always in pleasant awe when a new life is born. Be it a kit or a colt, a lamb or a kid, or even the first green shoot of corn . . . there is a sanctity in new life that I believe all farmers hold fervent.

I recollect one particular calf.

We named him Calvin, in honor of Vermont's only President of the United States, Calvin Coolidge. Like almost all Vermont folk, President Coolidge was a good solid Republican.

Winter Calf

I was fast asleep. But somehow heard
my mother's voice, and her quickened word:
"Ruthie's time is come, get to your clothes!"
And from the bedded depths of quilts I rose.

My bare feet danced across the floor
to the window white with frosty hoar;
to see the winter night, so black and dead.
A lantern yellowed deep inside the shed.

Sockless toes in boots, I could not care.
I ran from chamber down the winding stair
and to the door, and fast across the yard
out to the shed, where Ruthie's breath came hard.

Inside the shed, her labor fought the cold.
"Too old," my Papa said, "she's just too old
to calf." His face was darkened in a frown.
"She's weak with trying." She was lying down.

Kneeling in the straw I scratched her ear
just to let her know that we were near.
I tore the rags and hung them on a peg.
Papa lifted high her free hind leg.

The straw beneath her now was sticky red,
"Try it now, old girl," my Papa said
to Ruthie, as she heaved inside the pen.
Her heavy belly strained and strained again.

The labor finally opened up her rump.
I fetched a pail of water from the pump
and with a rag I wiped her muzzle cool,
while Papa larged her with his cutting tool.

Ruthie lathered up. She sweat a lot;
her trembling hide was wet and steaming hot
from labor. It was weak and painful slow,
but the head of Ruthie's calf began to show.

Her soft brown eyes were bulged. I guess the strain
made her eyes do that, and also pain.
The borning split her loins almost in half,
as with one valiant push she had her calf.

As a proud young flag of life unfurled,
out he came. Into a winter world,
shaking like a leaf and soaking wet.
We dried him with our rags and gave him pet.

But Ruthie did not even raise a horn.
"She's gone," said Papa, "but her calf is born."
Tired now, I fell into my bed.
A winter calf lay warm out in the shed.

IRONIC, that humankind is the only critter on Earth that was blessed (or cursed) with the gift of self-awareness. Yet we are the only varmits who can't accept ourselves. Maybe that's why most of us are so ornery. Happiness is knowing what you are.

You can learn more about Principle just by watching an inchworm for five minutes, than reading philosophy (especially mine) for an all day. Bugs and birds and beasts seem to know what they are, where they're headed, plus what to do when they get to it.

When I think of the animal kingdom on our Vermont farm alone, I am grateful to the Giver for providing such a wide and worthy faculty for my early education. Papa read little and wrote less. Yet he remains in my memory as the most sophisticated man I ever pleasured to work beside. Haven Peck knew what he was: a farmer, a father, a friend and neighbor, who believed in the world that God had made. And laughed at man's interpretation.

"Niagara Falls," he said, "was meant to go downhill, not up." Papa never saw those falls, but he sure saw the rightness in the few meager acres that he worked all his life and finally got dropped to rest in. Small, but it was one heck of a good farm. Good critters, too.

Feet

Behind the barn in meadow rill
Pants a taffy Jersey bull.
The sheep are grazing on the hill;
By rocks are gray round rocks of wool.

Our sow is lying, feeding young,
Not looking at the summer sky.
A milkcow chews, unhurried one,
And whips her tail to shoo a fly.

A goat is eating cabbage grounds,
Not caring that the hornets hum.
The mare inside her stable pounds
Her shoe against the floorboard drum.

By the hearth my dog may nap.
Four-footed animals I knew.
A cat is purring in my lap,
And poems are four-footed, too.

PAPA used to say, "It pays
to be honest; but for most folks, it don't pay
enough."

So much of survival is just plain thievery. And
that sure did apply to us Pecks. It was joyous to
discover a cache of hickory nuts that was put-by

for winter by a squirrel. We'd partly rob his storehouse. Just as surely as we'd rob a pig that stores up food in his own fat, until butchery usurps it. Not because we need the flesh, but because we want it. The word *need* is often a shabby excuse, as some wanton fool is too dishonest to admit that he *wants*.

I want a pork roast. Even though I do not need it, I will kill to get it. Sometimes, however, our raids on the treasure chests of our fellow critters turned out to be frolic as well as food.

Bee Tree

Jacob Thatcher, out of breath from
running down from his next farm . . .
through the woods to our place, yelled
to Papa, "Hey! I found me one!"

"Just one?" spoke Papa, looking up
not even once, while mending on
the harness our mare Betsy broke
when a rabbit up and shied her.

"Bee tree," Mr. Thatcher said,
"I was fixing fence this morning
just up the hollow when I heard it
bumbling music, sweet as honey."

I disrecall that I'd heard Mr.
Thatcher put two words together
more than twice. And once was when
his barn was fired. He was anxious.

"That so? That so, Jake?" said Papa,
drawing up a buckle trace
right and snug fit. "Well?" said Jacob,
much more in his character.

"Boy!" said I, "do I like honey."
But neither even looked my way.
I was about to add "on pancakes,"
but instead I held my tongue.

"Swarming?" Papa said to Mr.
Thatcher. "No," said Jacob, "settled
down and queened for sure. You coming?"
Papa spit and thought a bit.

"I'll come," said Papa. "Split the sugar
fifty you and fifty me."
"But you got only seven people,"
Jacob said, "and we got ten."

"Maybe so," said Papa, thinking
for a minute. Then he poked me
in the ribs. "But wager this one
here'll eat four times his share."

"Agreed," said Jacob, looking dark
to me. So Papa went to fetch
an axe, and one for Jacob, too,
and rags and then a ball of string.

The bee tree was a hickory
long dead, and shorn of upper limbs,
just like a lonely person; but
with apiary up inside.

Papa ragged my face so I
could hardly see a thing. He tied
my trousers to my legs and said
to keep my hands inside my pockets.

The first axe blow sent bees a flying
out so soon the air was black
as soot, as when we clean the fire
chimney when the winter's over.

And buzz! It surely was amazing
how those honey bees could sing
the very same high note. The more
they chopped, the more the bees sang on.

Jacob made the undercut, as
Papa cut the yonder side.
Each axe took its equal turn,
and I'd say Papa's chips were bigger.

Breaking twice, the tree broke off,
crashing through the other trees
that stood nearby, and made the leaves
fly with the bees. It bounced and rested.

"It's hot," said Papa. But he couldn't
wipe his face, it being ragged
like mine and Mr. Thatcher's. Then we
walked down to the upper end.

Mr. Thatcher took a sting and
hollered out a word I had
never heard. And Papa looked at
Jacob Thatcher. It was nervous.

Papa, black with bees, and gloved,
poked a pole inside the hive
and pulled it out, all yellow rich
and ripe with sticky honey sugar.

Worker bees and warriors
were quick to surround the Queen,
protecting her royal majesty
from us. And that's when Mr.

Thatcher said he'd need to get
more honey-pails. "Besides, it's time
for dinner," Papa noticed, looking
at the sky. He said, "It's noon."

So we left our honey snug
and sound. We parted, home for dinner.
We later fetched four honey-pails
back to Mr. Thatcher's hollow.

"Wait here," said Papa, whispering
to me. "If Jacob comes, you bid
the same to him." He left me standing
in the brush and hurried on.

I disobeyed a bit and followed
him to see the tree. And there
she was! A young she-bear
in the honey, getting stung.

Her nose was swollen, snapping at
the bees. Her claws were white with wax.
She'd lick a paw and brush her face
and then tongue off the honey there.

So, before my father caught me
disobedient, I scampered
right back to the very place
he told me wait. And he came hurried.

Along came Jacob, toting seven
ten-quart pails. Through rags he saw
our empty honey-pails. Bewildered,
he was just about to question.

Papa said, "I wouldn't set foot
in there, I be you." But Mr.
Thatcher didn't say an utter,
but departed all the same.

Papa smiled (a rare occasion)
and we retreated from the hollow
toward our place. On reaching home,
we looked back yonder, heard commotion.

The bushes parted, Mr. Thatcher
came out faster than he'd entered.
For good reason. He was being
heeled upon by that she-bear.

It would be my judgment Mr.
Thatcher, he could run about
as fast as any man his age
could do. Which wasn't very fast.

But running downhill, Mr. Thatcher
held his lead. Because a bear's
hind legs are longer and so therefore
can't run down as well as up.

Down our pasture, Mr. Thatcher
ran with honey-pails all banging
in the air. And yelling every
step enough to scare Old Ned.

But he didn't scare the bear.
An apple tree stood near the creek,
while Mr. Thatcher hurried up,
clanking pails and all, to safety.

"Get much sugar, Jake?" yelled Papa
up to Mr. Thatcher, who was
shouting down to Papa, 'bout a
gun. The she-bear waited under.

Papa's grin I thought would almost
split his face. He took a stick and
beat the bottom of his pail
and yelled. The young she-bear retreated.

Back she rambled, toward the hollow
where the bee tree was. And Mr.
Thatcher climbed him down the
apple tree and limped on home.

Papa always mirthed about that
bee tree. Called it "Jacob's bear."
He never let that story die,
and told it often. So do I.

Final Stone

YOU'RE a friend, old reader.

I owe that to you now. Because you persevered enough to squint this long in a book that rambles around like a crooked Vermont cowpath and doesn't seem to go anywhere.

But hold on. Come to think of it, a cowpath always goes somewhere. To a barn, to a freshet of cool water, to a puddle of shade beneath a meadow elm. Cows do know where they want to go. Better yet, they usual get there. And I guess that applies to this farmer friend of yours who has the salt to attempt poetry. At least we got to the end of the book, you and I.

It's a short book. Yet all my books are brief. Some say my novels pull up short and end too quickly. Well, to such a plaintiff I shall defend by calling my mother, Lucy Peck, as a witness. Mama always said, way back before I was old enough to digest her wisdom, that "Not quite enough is the right amount."

You know, the more I study on that little old statement, the sounder it blooms. Why, you can apply that to love as well as laughter. Leave your lover wanting more of you. Leave your audience (if you're a clown) craving more antics of your wit. Leave your hosts while they are still warmed by the coals of your company. Leave your mate each day, as did the hunter with his club, yet return to your cave at sundown. Your mate and your young will welcome you.

Times change? No, only dates change.

Earthy Reason remains the same. It is Law. It is Principle. Years ago, a would-be attorney served as a clerk to an established lawyer. Instead of attending a law school, he read the law, and then took the bar exam. You don't have to be a scholar to read the land, to enrich yourself with its reason. You need not be a man of letters to be a man of learning.

As I wrote early on, I want to share with you the few flecks of knowledge that the land has afforded me.

Most of all, I enjoy talking to you on these pages. Not to you as an author to a reader, but more like a friend to a neighbor. I give you not wine, but well water. You may judge "how shallow it is." True enough. But it is mine, at least. I hauled it up in the oak of my own bucket.

And if my water is too hard, too mineral and muddy for your taste, then you are free to sip elsewhere. But if my water can cool your thirst for plain philosophy or homely beauty or simple understanding, from a well deep in Vermont earth, then you may drink your fill from my dipper, my friend.

Final Stone

I fit the final stone into my wall
With some regret, because my work is through.
The stone fence that I built's not very tall,
It never may be seen from neighbor's view.

Will my fence stand, as other fences stood,
To stand the test of time upon this land?
I've done the best I can; I think it should,
Each stone was shapen carefully by hand.

I did not borrow mortar or the stone;
But took it from my very property,
So I can say with pride it is my own—
This wall I built, that only I can see.

Its line is true, and plain as Yankee sense.
I fit the final stone into my fence.